EASTER

The Easter Story Wreath

Celebrate the story of Easter by creating a colorful wreath that explains the last week of Jesus' life including His entrance into Jerusalem, the Last Supper, Jesus praying in the Garden of Gethsemane, the crucifixion, and the Resurrection. Read the Easter story together as a family and then display the wreath for family and friends to enjoy.

Materials Needed:

- Patterns on pages 21, 22, 23
- Crayons or markers
- Scissors
- Construction paper
- Glue

Instructions:

- Color the patterns on pages 21, 22, and 23 with crayons or markers.
- Cut out the colored patterns.
- Take a large 12" x 12" square piece of construction paper (any matching color) and cut around edges to make a circle.
- Cut a circle in the center to make a wreath.
- Glue the patterns to the circle as shown in the picture below.

Helpful Hint: Use a paper plate or round bowl as an outline and trace the circle on the construction paper first.

EASTER

The Jelly Bean Prayer Jar

Materials Needed:

- Pattern on page 24
- Scissors
- Mason jar
- Ribbon
- Hole punch
- Jelly beans
- Piece of fabric

Instructions:

- Cut out "The Jelly Bean Prayer" on page 24.
- Hole punch the top left corner.
- Fill the mason jar with jelly beans.
- Cut out a piece of fabric to fit over the top of the mason jar.
- Wrap a ribbon around the top of the mason jar and through "The Jelly Bean Prayer" hole and tie securely.

Helpful Hint: If you don't have any fabric, just use the mason jar lid and tie the ribbon around the top of the lid.

Color Or Make Your Own Easter Wristbands

Materials Needed:

- Pattern on page 20
- Scissors
- Construction paper
- Tape or glue
- Markers

Instructions:

- Color patterns on page 20.
- Write "He Is Risen," or other Easter phrases on the blank strip to create your own wristband.
- Cut out the wristbands.
- Wrap around your wrist to determine a comfortable length to fit your wrist.
- Cut any extra material from both sides of the wristband.
- Put around your wrist and ask someone to help tape it closed.

Tissue Paper Cross

Materials Needed:

- Scissors
- Construction paper
- Glue
- Ribbon
- Hole punch

Instructions:

- Cut a cross shape out of construction paper.
- Hole punch the top in the center.
- Tie a ribbon through the hole to make a loop.
- Tear off small pieces of tissue paper and pinch them so the pieces stand up.
- Glue tissue paper pieces to the cross to fill up all of the space.

Great Lesson!

This is what God told us: God has given us eternal life, and this life is in his Son.
1 John 5:11 ICB

Easy Popsicle Stick Easter Crosses

Materials Needed:

- Popsicle sticks
- Glue
- Yarn
- Embellishments or glitter

Instructions:

- Take the popsicle sticks and glue to make a cross.
- Decorate the popsicle sticks as desired.

I Am A New Creation Butterfly

Materials Needed:

- Pattern on page 30
- Scissors
- Construction paper
- Glue
- Buttons
- Black pipe cleaner
- Egg carton

Instructions:

- Fold a piece of construction paper in half.
- Lay the wing pattern found on page 30 on the folded edge and trace.
- Cut out the butterfly pattern.
- Cut out three sections from an egg carton.
- Glue egg carton sections in the center of the butterfly and let dry.
- Decorate the butterfly with jewels, circles, buttons, pipe cleaners, or any materials as desired.

Great Lesson!

If anyone belongs to Christ, then he is made new. The old things have gone; everything is made new!
2 Corinthians 5:17 ICB

"I Am The Vine" Button Craft

Materials Needed:

- Template on page 25
- Scissors
- Brown, washable paint
- Construction paper
- Glue
- Buttons

Instructions:

- Paint a tree using brown, washable paint.
- Decorate the tree by gluing on colorful buttons. Make sure to leave the area by the tree trunk undecorated for the verse to be glued on last.
- Cut out the "I Am The Vine" pattern on page 25.
- Glue the pattern to a piece of construction paper.
- Cut it out so the verse is framed by construction paper.
- Glue the framed verse to the trunk of the tree.
- Frame the picture as desired or tack up on a bulletin board.

SUMMER FUN

"God Keeps His Promises" Pipe Cleaner Rainbow

Materials Needed:

- Colored pipe cleaners
- Blue or white foam pieces
- Scissors
- Glue or glue dots
- Tape
- Pencil
- Paper

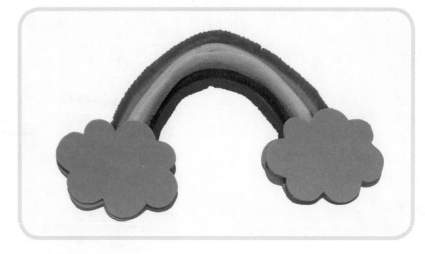

Instructions:

- Take a piece of paper and draw a cloud pattern on it.
- Cut out the pattern and use it to draw clouds on the foam pieces. You'll need 4 clouds.
- Cut out the foam clouds.
- Place the pipe cleaners in color order (as shown) and tape them to the front of the cloud.
  The colors are red, orange, yellow, green, blue, indigo, and violet.
- Bend the pipe cleaners to make a rainbow and tape to another cloud.
- Place the 2 remaining clouds on the top covering up the tape and then secure with glue or glue dots.

Great Lesson!

"I am putting my rainbow in the clouds. It is the sign of the agreement between me and the earth. When I bring clouds over the earth, a rainbow appears in the clouds. Then I will remember my agreement. It is between me and you and every living thing. Floodwaters will never again destroy all life on the earth. When the rainbow appears in the clouds, I will see it. Then I will remember the agreement that continues forever. It is between me and every living thing on the earth." Genesis 9:13-16 ICB

Armor Of God

Materials Needed:

- Patterns on pages 30 and 31
- Scissors
- Markers, crayons, or colored pencils

Instructions:

- Cut out the boy or girl pattern on page 31.
- Color and cut out each piece of armor on page 30.
- Glue each piece of armor onto the boy or girl pattern in the correct order.
- Read Ephesians 6:10-17.

Paul tells us to be strong in the Lord and in His mighty power by putting on the full armor of God.

1. **Breastplate of Righteousness**
2. **Belt of Truth**
3. **Helmet of Salvation**
4. **Gospel of Peace**
5. **Sword of the Spirit**
6. **Shield of Faith**

SUMMER FUN

"Learn The Old Testament Books Of The Bible"

Materials Needed:

- Pattern on page 24
- Markers or crayons
- Scissors
- Tape
- Glue
- Paper picture frame
- Clothespins
- Embellishments

Instructions:

- Color then cut out the pattern on page 24.
- Tape the pattern to the back of a picture mat or frame so the design shows through.
- Write the names of the books of the Bible on clothespins. See list below.
- Decorate clothespins with embellishments.
- Pin the clothespins around the outside of the picture mat or frame.

Memorize the books of the Bible with music!
To download the song "I'm Gonna Learn The Books Of The Bible" and a PDF of this book, visit **www.musicforlearning.com** and enter the **promo code**

OLDT39

The Old Testament

Genesis	1 Kings	Ecclesiastes	Obadiah
Exodus	2 Kings	Song of Songs	Jonah
Leviticus	1 Chronicles	Isaiah	Micah
Numbers	2 Chronicles	Jeremiah	Nahum
Deuteronomy	Ezra	Lamentations	Habakkuk
Joshua	Nehemiah	Ezekiel	Zephaniah
Judges	Esther	Daniel	Haggai
Ruth	Job	Hosea	Zechariah
1 Samuel	Psalms	Joel	Malachi
2 Samuel	Proverbs	Amos	

Helpful Hint: After making the craft, sing along with the song and point to each clothespin to make learning the books of the Bible easy and fun!

SUMMER FUN

"Worship The Lord With Gladness"
Tambourine Craft

Materials Needed:

- Pattern on page 26
- Ribbon
- Scissors
- Glue
- Paper plates
- Hole punch
- Buttons, beans, or other filler
  that will make noise

Instructions:

- Color and cut out the pattern on page 26.
- Glue it to the bottom of a paper plate.
- Put 2 paper plates together with top
  rims facing each other.
- Hole punch together so the holes line up.
- Take the bottom plate and put filler on the plate.
- Put the other plate on top, matching up the holes.
- Thread ribbon through the paper plates around
  the edges first to make sure the plates are attached
  to each other and the buttons or beans do not fall out.
- Next tie ribbon through each hole to make fringe around
  the paper plate, further securing the plates together.

Helpful Hint: Use a heavier paper plate to ensure the tambourine lasts longer with vigorous shaking.

Color Your Own
Water Bottle Labels

Materials Needed:

- Patterns on page 32
- Scissors
- Markers, crayons, or colored pencils
- Tape
- Water bottles

Instructions:

- Color then cut out the patterns on page 32.
- Tape the pattern around a water bottle to decorate.

THANKSGIVING

"I Am Thankful For..." Placemat

Materials Needed:
- Large piece of brown construction paper
- Black marker
- Pencil or pen

Helpful Hint: Any color of construction paper will work. Use red, yellow, orange, or another color that matches your Thanksgiving Day table!

Instructions:
- Write "I am Thankful for..." on a piece of construction paper the size of a placemat.
- Draw lines under the words.
- Leave a pencil or pen by each place setting so everyone can write down what they are thankful for.
- Share your thoughts around the Thanksgiving table.

Silverware Holder

Materials Needed:
- Pattern on page 26
- Brown construction paper
- Glue

Instructions:
- Cut a 4" x 8" piece of construction paper.
- Fold 3½" from the bottom and glue the ends, leaving the middle section open.
- Cut out the pattern on page 26 and glue to the center of the silverware holder. Let dry.
- Place a folded napkin in the holder and add silverware, as shown in the picture.

THANKSGIVING

Family Prayer Jar

Materials Needed:

- Pattern on page 25
- Scissors
- Markers, crayons, or colored pencils
- Tape
- Mason Jar
- Paper

Instructions:

- Color and cut out the pattern on page 25.
- Tape around a mason jar.
- Write prayer requests on strips of paper and fill the prayer jar. Read prayer requests as a family before bedtime and pray together.

Prayer Starters:

Dear God,
Thank You for all of Your blessings.
Amen.

Dear God,
Thank You for forgiving me when I do not do the right thing. I love you!
Amen.

Dear Jesus,
We love You and worship only You.
Amen.

Dear God,
Thank You for watching over me and keeping me safe.
Amen.

Dear Jesus,
Thank You for being with me when I am afraid.
Amen.

Dear Jesus,
Thank You for being my friend.
Amen.

**Dear God,
Thank You for keeping Your promises.
Amen.**

Dear God,
Thank You for creating me just as I am.
Amen.

Dear God,
Thank You for being loving and faithful.
Amen.

Dear Jesus,
Thank You for listening to me when I talk to You.
Amen.

Dear God,
Thank You that I am Your child.
Amen.

Dear God,
Thank You for Your Son, Jesus.
Amen.

Dear God,
Please help (name). We know You hear us when we pray to You.
Amen.

Dear God,
Thank You for…
Amen.

THANKSGIVING

Pipe Cleaner Napkin Holder

Materials Needed:

- Pipe cleaners
- Googly eyes
- Orange and brown construction paper
- Paper napkins
- Glue

Instructions:

- Cut a 2" strip of brown construction paper and lay flat.
- Loop pipe cleaners to form turkey feathers and glue to the brown paper making a multi-colored turkey.
- Take a brown pipe cleaner and loop into a solid circle to form a turkey face.
- Glue the brown pipe cleaner circle on top of the other pipe cleaners.
- Decorate with googly eyes.
- Cut a triangle out of the orange construction paper for the beak. Glue beak beneath eyes.
- Make a loop with the brown construction paper and tape closed.
- Fold napkin to fit inside the loop.

"Lord, I Am Thankful For..." Pumpkin Craft

Materials Needed:

- Pattern on page 17
- Orange and brown construction paper
- Scissors
- Markers, crayons, or colored pencils
- Magazines or newspapers

Instructions:

- Cut out pattern on page 17.
- Trace and cut out 2 pumpkins on orange construction paper.
- Cut the second pumpkin as shown in the picture to create a pocket.
- Glue the edges of pumpkins and let dry.
- Write *Lord, I am thankful for...* on the front in marker.
- Draw and color, or cut out from magazines, things you are thankful for and place them in the pocket.

CHRISTMAS

Popsicle Stick Christmas Story Ornament

Materials Needed:
- Patterns on page 21
- Popsicle sticks
- Scissors
- Glue
- Markers, crayons, or colored pencils

Instructions:
- Color and cut out the patterns on page 21.
- Glue a popsicle stick on the top and on the bottom of the picture as shown.
- Next glue popsicle sticks on each side.
- Glue the verse to the bottom of the frame.
- Make a loop with yarn and tape securely on the top of the ornament.
- Hang on a Christmas tree or as a decoration in your home.

Popsicle Stick Manger

Materials Needed:
- Tissues
- Popsicle sticks
- Straw basket filler
- Glue
- Miniature plastic baby

Instructions:
- Take two popsicle sticks and glue them together to make a V for the manger legs. Make two of these.
- Glue popsicle sticks side by side to make the base of the manger as shown in the picture.
- Glue straw onto the top of the cradle. Let dry.
- Wrap the plastic baby in tissues.
- Place baby in the manger.

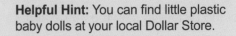

Helpful Hint: You can find little plastic baby dolls at your local Dollar Store.

Candy Cane Poem

Materials Needed:

- Pattern on page 26
- Scissors
- Pipe cleaner
- Red and white beads
- Ribbon
- Hole punch
- Markers, crayons, or colored pencils

Instructions:

- Thread the pipe cleaner with red and white beads and bend the pipe cleaner into the shape of a candy cane.
- Color and cut out the pattern on page 26.
- Hole punch the top left corner of the pattern.
- Thread a ribbon through the hole and tie it into a bow around the candy cane.

Helpful Hint: You can also buy candy canes and tie the poems to them for quick and easy Christmas presents.

Popsicle Stick Photo Ornament

Materials Needed:

- Photo
- Popsicle sticks
- Embellishments
- Glitter
- Ribbon
- Glue

Instructions:

- Glue popsicle sticks to make a frame.
- Fold the ribbon to make a loop and glue to the back center of the frame.
- Cut the picture to fit in the frame and glue in the back over the ribbon.
- Decorate as desired.

Bow Wreath

Materials Needed:

- Package of self-stick bows
- One large bow
- Cardboard
- Wreath hanger or ribbon

Instructions:

- Cut a large circle about three inches wide out of cardboard.
- Affix bows to wreath.
- Place a bow on the bottom of the wreath (as shown) if desired.
- Hang wreath over a door with a wreath hanger or ribbon.

Helpful Hint: If bows are not self-stick, they can be taped or glued to the cardboard.

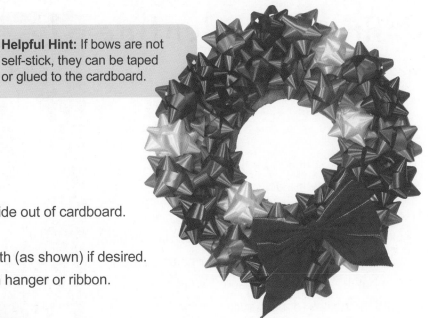

Snowman Donuts

Materials Needed:

- Powdered donuts
- Carrots
- Chocolate chips or candy-coated chocolate pieces
- Mini chocolate chips

Instructions:

- Cut carrots for the nose and place in center of each donut (use pre-cut carrots if desired).
- Use chocolate chips for the eyes.
- Use mini chocolate chips for the mouth.

Gumdrop Tree

Materials Needed:

- 2 (14.5 oz.) bags of gumdrops
- Toothpicks
- Styrofoam cone
- Tape
- Scissors

Instructions:

- Stick one toothpick into each gumdrop. Starting at the top of the cone, push gumdrops into Styrofoam in a line from top to bottom.
- Repeat until the entire cone is covered in gumdrops.

Helpful Hint: Cut out a paper star and tape to a toothpick. Stick star in top gumdrop.

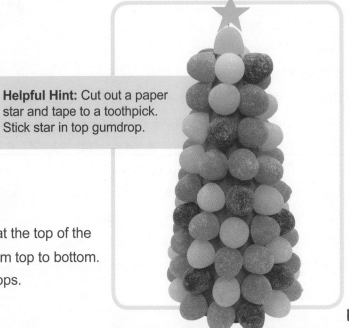

John 3:16 Valentine

Materials Needed:

- Pattern on page 29
- Scissors
- Glue
- Colored construction paper or a red and white doily

Instructions:

- Glue doilies (or heart-shaped construction paper cutouts) together with the smaller heart on top.
- Cut out the pattern from page 29 and glue it onto the doilies (or construction paper).

Helpful Hint: You can purchase a pack of 24 red doilies and 16 larger pink doilies at your local dollar store.

Valentine Love Angel

Materials Needed:

- Patterns on pages 28 and 29
- Scissors
- Tape
- Colored construction paper
- Crayons, markers, or colored pencils
- Glue
- Glitter Glue (optional)
- Ribbons (optional)
- Heart stickers (optional)

Instructions:

- Color angel's head and arms on page 28 and cut out.
- Cut out the half circle and trace onto a piece of construction paper.
- Cut out the shape and roll into a cone. Tape together in the back.
- Cut out the heart pattern on page 29 and trace two hearts onto construction paper.
- Cut out hearts and tape them to the back of the cone to make wings for the angel.
- Glue the arms onto each side of the cone.
- Glue the angel's head to the top of the cone.
- Cut out the scripture heart on page 28 and glue it to the front of the angel.
- Decorate as you wish!

VALENTINE

Valentine's Day Handprint Poem

Materials Needed:

- Pattern on page 27
- Nontoxic paint
- Large paintbrush
- Colored construction paper
- Glue
- Lined paper
- Paper plate

Instructions:

- Pour paint onto paper plate.
- Use paintbrush to paint child's hands. Have child press their painted hands onto construction paper.
- While the handprints dry, have older children write the Valentine poem on lined paper and glue to construction paper.

Other Variation: For younger children, cut out the pattern on page 27 and glue below the handprints.

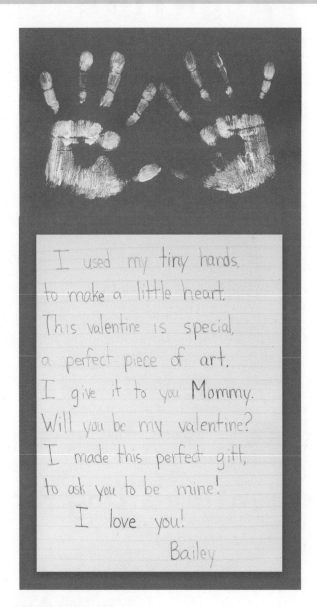

Easy Valentine's Day Card Bags

Materials Needed:

- Pattern on page 27
- Scissors
- Glue
- Crayons, markers, or colored pencils
- Paper bags

Instructions:

- Color and cut out the bear pattern on page 27.
- Glue bear to the bag.
- Write your name in the heart.
- Decorate the bag as you wish.

Helpful Hint: Valentine's Day bags can be found at your local dollar store.

Valentine's Day Lollipop Candies

Materials Needed:

- Pattern on page 19
- Foam heart stickers
- Lollipops
- Heart candies (optional)
- Construction paper
- Scissors
- Glue

Instructions:

- Cut out wing pattern on page 19.
  Trace pattern onto construction paper and cut out.
- Write a Valentine message around the outside of the wings.
  For example, "Be my Valentine" or "Jesus is my Valentine."
- Cut slits on the dotted lines.
- Decorate wings with heart foam stickers.
- Glue on heart candies (optional).
- Slide lollipop stick through slits.

Valentine's Day Picture Frames

Materials Needed:

- Patterns on pages 18 and 19
- Construction paper
- Pipe cleaners
- Foam heart stickers
- Glue
- Scissors
- Magnets

Instructions:

- Color the hearts on pages 18 and 19,
  or cut them out to use as patterns.
- If using as patterns, trace the hearts on red
  or pink construction paper.
- Place and glue a picture in the center of the smaller heart.
- Decorate around the picture with additional red and pink hearts.
- Use foam stickers or heart-shaped candies
  to decorate the frame as desired.
- Glue magnets to the back of the frame and hang on the refrigerator.

"Lord, I Am Thankful For..." Pumpkin Craft

"Lord, I Am Thankful For..." Pumpkin Craft

Valentine's Day
Picture Frames

18

Valentine's Day
Picture Frames

Valentine's Day
Lollipop Candies

19

JESUS ♡ JESUS ♡ JESUS ♡ JESUS

FOR GOD SO LOVED THE WORLD 🌍

HE IS RISEN! HE IS RISEN!

HAPPY ✝ EASTER

I'M a FOLLOWER OF CHRIST

Mary gave birth to Jesus and wrapped Him in cloths and placed Him in a manger.

Popsicle Stick Christmas Story Ornament

The Easter Story Wreath

THE EASTER STORY

The Triumphal Entry
The next day the large crowd
that had come for the feast heard that
Jesus was on his way to Jerusalem. So they took
branches from palm trees and went out to meet him.
They shouted, "Hosanna!" "Blessed is the one
who comes in the name of the Lord!"
"Blessed is the king of Israel!"
John 12:12-13 NIRV

Jesus' Crucifixion
He had to carry his own cross. He went
out to a place called the Skull. In the Aramaic
language it was called Golgotha. There they nailed
Jesus to the cross. Two other men were crucified
with him. One was on each side of him.
Jesus was in the middle.
John 19:17-18 NIRV

The Garden of Gethsemane
Then Jesus went with his disciples to a place
called Gethsemane. He said to them, "Sit here while
I go over there and pray." He went a little farther.
Then he fell with his face to the ground. He prayed,
"My Father, if it is possible, take this cup of suffering
away from me. But let what you want be done,
not what I want."
Matthew 26:36, 39 NIRV

Jesus' Resurrection
The Sabbath day was now over. It was dawn
on the first day of the week. Mary Magdalene and
the other Mary went to look at the tomb. There was a
powerful earthquake. An angel of the Lord came down
from heaven. The angel went to the tomb. He rolled
back the stone and sat on it. His body shone like
lightning. His clothes were as white as snow.
Matthew 28:1-3 NIRV

The Last Supper
While they were eating, Jesus took bread.
He gave thanks and broke it. He handed it to his
disciples and said, "Take this and eat it. This is my body."
Then he took a cup. He gave thanks and handed it
to them. He said, "All of you drink from it. This is
my blood of the covenant. It is poured out to
forgive the sins of many people."
Matthew 26:26-28 NIRV

He Is Risen!
The angel said to the women,
"Don't be afraid. I know that you are looking
for Jesus, who was crucified. He is not here! He has
risen, just as he said he would! Come and see the place
where he was lying. Go quickly! Tell his disciples, 'He
has risen from the dead. He is going ahead of you
into Galilee. There you will see him.'
Now I have told you."
Matthew 28:5-7 NIRV

The Easter Story Wreath

AS FOR
me and my
FAMILY
we will
SERVE
the LORD

Joshua 24:15 ICB

The Jelly Bean Prayer Jar

THE JELLY
BEAN PRAYER

Red is for the blood Jesus shed.

Green is for new life ahead.

Black is for the sins we've made.

White is for perfect grace He gave.

Yellow is for the beautiful sunlight.

Orange is for the edge of night.

Purple is for His hour of sorrow.

Pink is for our new tomorrow.

©2017 Twin Sisters IP, LLC

Family Prayer Jar

♡ FAMILY PRAYER JAR

Here is what we can be sure of when we come to God in prayer. If we ask anything in keeping with what he wants, he hears us.

1 John 5:14 NIRV

"I Am The Vine" Button Craft

"I am the vine, and you are the branches. If a person remains in me and I remain in him, then he produces much fruit. But without me he can do nothing."

John 15:5 ICB

Silverware Holder

LORD, I will give *thanks* to you with all my *heart.*

Psalm 9:1 NIRV

Candy Cane Poem

Look at the candy cane, what do you see?
Stripes that are red like the blood shed for me.
White for my Savior who's sinless and pure!
"J" is for Jesus, My Lord, that's for sure!
Turn it around and a staff you will see
Jesus my shepherd is coming for me!

"Worship The Lord With Gladness" Tambourine Craft

WORSHIP the LORD with GLADNESS come to him with SONGS OF JOY

Psalm 100:2 NIRV

26

I used my tiny hands

to make a little heart.

This Valentine is special,

a perfect piece of art.

I give it to You, Jesus.

Will You be my valentine?

I made this perfect gift

to ask You to be mine!

**Valentine's Day
Handprint Poem**

**Easy Valentine's Day
Card Bags**

Valentine Love Angel

Love the LORD your God
with all your heart
and with all your soul
and with all your strength.
Deuteronomy 6:5 NIV

Valentine
Love Angel

John 3:16 Valentine

For God so loVed the world
That He gAve
His onLy
BegottEn
So oNly
ThaT whoever
Believes In Him
Should Not perish
But have Everlasting
Life.

John 3:16 NKJV

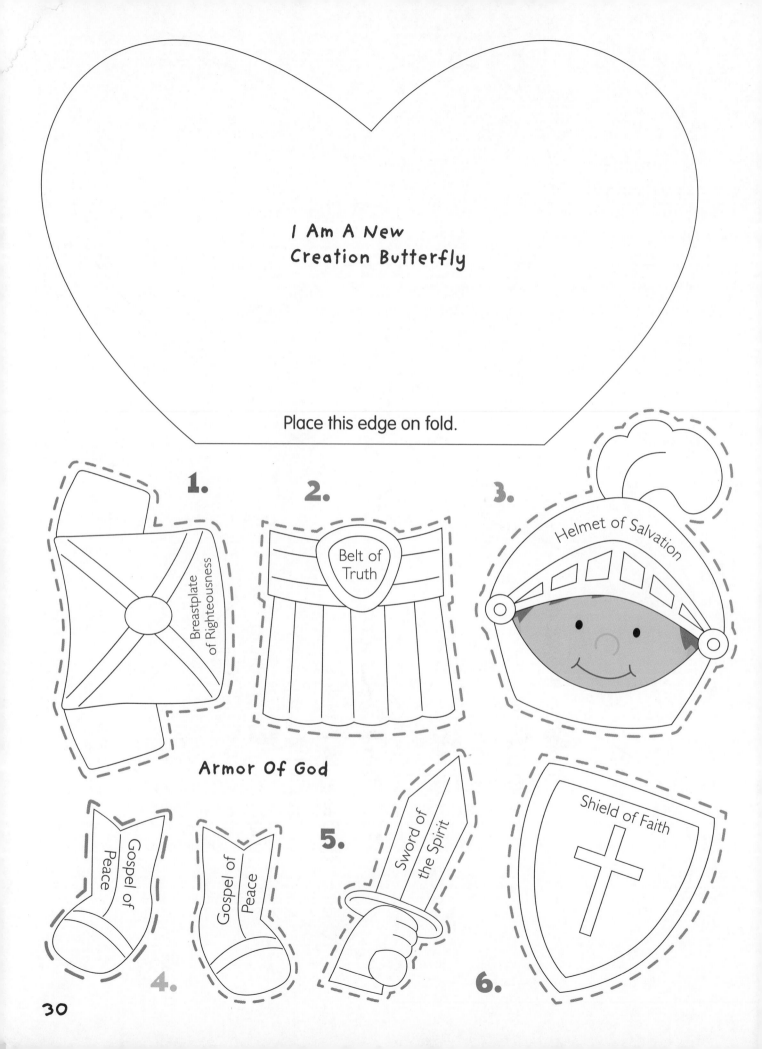

I Am A New
Creation Butterfly

Place this edge on fold.

1.

Breastplate of Righteousness

2.

Belt of Truth

3.

Helmet of Salvation

Armor Of God

Gospel of Peace

Gospel of Peace

4.

5.

Sword of the Spirit

Shield of Faith

6.

THIRST AFTER JESUS

"But anyone who drinks the water I give will never be thirsty again." John 4:14 ERV

"BUT ANYONE WHO DRINKS THE WATER I GIVE WILL NEVER BE THIRSTY AGAIN." JOHN 4:14 ERV

THIRST AFTER JESUS

THIRST AFTER JESUS

"BUT ANYONE WHO DRINKS THE WATER I GIVE WILL NEVER BE THIRSTY AGAIN." JOHN 4:14 ERV